INCLUSIVE EDUCATION WITH DIFFERENTIATED INSTRUCTION FOR CHILDREN WITH DISABILITIES
A GUIDANCE NOTE

OCTOBER 2022

ASIAN DEVELOPMENT BANK

 Creative Commons Attribution 3.0 IGO license (CC BY 3.0 IGO)

© 2022 Asian Development Bank
6 ADB Avenue, Mandaluyong City, 1550 Metro Manila, Philippines
Tel +63 2 8632 4444; Fax +63 2 8636 2444
www.adb.org

Some rights reserved. Published in 2022.

ISBN 978-92-9269-779-2 (print), 978-92-9269-780-8 (electronic), 978-92-9269-781-5 (ebook)
Publication Stock No. TIM220450
DOI: http://dx.doi.org/10.22617/TIM220450

The views expressed in this publication are those of the authors and do not necessarily reflect the views and policies of the Asian Development Bank (ADB) or its Board of Governors or the governments they represent.

ADB does not guarantee the accuracy of the data included in this publication and accepts no responsibility for any consequence of their use. The mention of specific companies or products of manufacturers does not imply that they are endorsed or recommended by ADB in preference to others of a similar nature that are not mentioned.

By making any designation of or reference to a particular territory or geographic area, or by using the term "country" in this document, ADB does not intend to make any judgments as to the legal or other status of any territory or area.

This work is available under the Creative Commons Attribution 3.0 IGO license (CC BY 3.0 IGO) https://creativecommons.org/licenses/by/3.0/igo/. By using the content of this publication, you agree to be bound by the terms of this license. For attribution, translations, adaptations, and permissions, please read the provisions and terms of use at https://www.adb.org/terms-use#openaccess.

This CC license does not apply to non-ADB copyright materials in this publication. If the material is attributed to another source, please contact the copyright owner or publisher of that source for permission to reproduce it. ADB cannot be held liable for any claims that arise as a result of your use of the material.

Please contact pubsmarketing@adb.org if you have questions or comments with respect to content, or if you wish to obtain copyright permission for your intended use that does not fall within these terms, or for permission to use the ADB logo.

Corrigenda to ADB publications may be found at http://www.adb.org/publications/corrigenda.

Note:
In this report, "$" refers to United States dollars.

Cover design by Ingrid Shroder.

CONTENTS

Acknowledgments	iv
Abbreviations	v
Glossary	vi
Executive Summary	viii

I. INTRODUCTION — 1

II. METHODOLOGY — 3
- Inclusive Education—A Global Definition — 3
- Challenges in Implementing Inclusive Education at the Country Level — 5

III. GUIDANCE FOR INCLUSIVE EDUCATION — 7
- Commitment to International Declarations and Policies — 7
- Development of National Legislation and Policies — 7
- Utilization of a Twin-Tracked Approach — 8
- Utilization of Differentiated Instruction — 9
- Screening and Identification Programs — 10
- Capacity Building on Inclusive Education — 12
- Ensuring Safety and Security of Learning Environments — 13
- Disability-Friendly Curriculum and Resources — 14
- Provision of Support Services for Families of Children with Disabilities — 18
- Encouragement of Partnership Approaches — 19
- Designing an Inclusive Education Project — 21

IV. CONCLUSIONS AND RECOMMENDATIONS — 23

Bibliography — 29

ACKNOWLEDGMENTS

This publication was authored by Asian Development Bank (ADB) consultants Eila Heikkilä and Bethany Davidson-Widby. The authors wish to express their gratitude and appreciation to Jukka Tulivuori, social sector specialist and program lead, Education Sector Group, Sustainable Development and Climate Change Department (SDCC), ADB, whose suggestions and encouragement helped in the better execution of this publication.

The technical assistance team would like to express gratitude to everyone who participated in this study and shared their valuable insights from the three ADB developing member countries—the Kyrgyz Republic, the Republic of the Marshall Islands, and Nepal.

The team also thanks ADB for its support in the technical assistance project. Special thanks also goes to Deepali Kapoor, inclusive education specialist, Pratham India; Maria Kett, associate professor, University College London; Malika Shagazatova, social development specialist, Gender Equality Thematic Group, SDCC, ADB; Gohar Tadevosyan, senior social development specialist, East Asia Department, ADB; and Naomi Thompson, project manager, Global Disability Innovation Hub. Thanks also goes to Kevin Corbin, education specialist, Central and West Asia Department, ADB; Smita Gyawali, senior project officer, Nepal Resident Mission, ADB; and Per Börjegren, senior education specialist, Pacific Department, ADB, for their continuous support during the study, as well as all who have provided their valuable comments and support for this guidance note.

Support in the finalization of this publication was provided by Dorothy Geronimo, senior education officer, SDCC, ADB, in close collaboration with April-Marie Gallega, publishing product coordinator, Department of Communications, ADB, and Maria Theresa Mercado, editorial consultant.

This publication would not have been produced without the encouragement and overall guidance of Brajesh Panth, chief, Education Sector Group, SDCC, ADB.

ABBREVIATIONS

ADB	–	Asian Development Bank
COVID-19	–	coronavirus disease
CWDs	–	children with disabilities
DMC	–	developing member country
ECEC	–	early childhood education and care
EMIS	–	education management information system
FGD	–	focus group discussion
ICT	–	information and communication technology
IEP	–	individual education plan
TA	–	technical assistance
TVET	–	technical and vocational education and training
UN	–	United Nations
UN CRPD	–	United Nations Convention on the Rights of Persons with Disabilities
UNESCO	–	United Nations Educational, Scientific and Cultural Organization
UNICEF	–	United Nations Children's Fund
USAID	–	United States Agency for International Development
WHO	–	World Health Organization

GLOSSARY

assistive technology and devices	–	A term for assistive, adaptive, and rehabilitative devices for people with disabilities.
child-centered approach	–	In a child-centered approach, a child can make decisions on his or her learning, and is not directed by a teacher. A child can take responsibility and choose what he or she will explore and learn.
differentiation of content	–	The knowledge, understanding, and skills that students need to learn. While learning goals remain the same for all students, differentiation of content allows students the opportunity to master the knowledge and skills within the range of their abilities. It answers the question: "What does the child need to learn?"
differentiation of process	–	How students understand and make sense of the content. The learning process utilizes different learning methods that address the individual needs of the learner (abilities, strengths, interests, preferences, motivation). It answers the question: "How does the child learn?"
differentiation of product	–	A student's learning outcomes (knowledge, understanding, skills). The learning outcomes can be presented and expressed in a variety of ways. It answers the question: "How are learning outcomes presented and assessed?"
differentiation of the learning environment	–	The modification of the learning environment to meet students' emotional needs. Examples of flexible learning spaces and elements are "quiet corners," lap desks, standing desks, and comfortable seating.
education management information system	–	An information management and data collection system to plan, monitor, and manage education development concerning different aspects and levels in education.

inclusive education	–	A strategy for including all children from gender, ethnic, and linguistic minorities, and with disabilities and learning difficulties, in mainstream education alongside peers in the same age group.
individual education plan	–	A plan that ensures individualized education, differentiated teaching and learning, and related support services adapted to the needs of a child with disabilities.
sector-wide approach	–	In a sector-wide approach, international development is planned and implemented in cooperation with governments, donors, and other stakeholders. Education development has joint objectives and programming (not single projects).
self-efficacy	–	One's belief in his or her abilities to perform effectively under certain situations. Teacher's self-efficacy is specific to the teaching profession in inclusive education.
twin-tracked approach	–	An approach where specialist support is provided for children with disabilities within the strategy of inclusion into mainstream education.

EXECUTIVE SUMMARY

Every child has the right to quality education in accordance with international policies. However, children with disabilities (CWDs) suffer disproportionately from exclusion from education, which has been exacerbated by the coronavirus disease (COVID-19) pandemic. Although CWDs represent only around 5% of the child population, they encompass more than half of out-of-school children globally. The aim of this guidance note is to support innovative policy and practice in inclusive education in developing member countries (DMCs) of the Asian Development Bank (ADB). It focuses in particular on the development of inclusive education with differentiated instruction to benefit CWDs in DMCs.

Inclusive education involves the understanding that all children have the right to quality education regardless of gender, disability, learning difficulty, ethnic or linguistic minority background, or any other personal feature. In inclusive education, CWDs learn alongside their age-based peers in mainstream education. The focus is on how to support all children, including CWDs, to learn successfully in inclusive education. The guidance note is based on international research and field study findings from three DMCs—the Kyrgyz Republic, the Republic of the Marshall Islands, and Nepal. Based on the findings, the guidance note presents key factors that are essential in the development of inclusive education systems, and teaching and learning practices.

There is a shared understanding that CWDs need to be ensured access to and inclusion in education starting from early childhood education and care (ECEC). Progression of CWDs from one education level to another needs to be supported to avoid dropout and exclusion. Students with disabilities need to be supported to reach the levels and qualifications of technical and vocational education and training (TVET) and higher education. To ensure equity in education, there is a methodological shift from the traditional "one-size-fits-all" model toward individualized teaching and learning practice in modern education.

The approach of differentiated instruction recognizes and supports all children, including CWDs, as individual learners in their age-based peer group. The aim is to increase every learner's educational opportunities, where teaching and learning processes are stimulated according to the learners' needs. In differentiated instruction, teaching is tailored to the needs and levels of CWDs in a way that maximizes benefits and avoids stigmatization.

In inclusive education, teaching methods and didactic approaches are designed according to individual requirements to motivate all children to master individual tasks and achieve learning outcomes successfully. A twin-tracked approach supports inclusion of all children in mainstream education and, at the same time, provides individualized and special support for learners with disabilities. Individualized teaching and learning approaches for CWDs include an individual education plan (IEP), adaptation of curricula, modification of teaching and learning methods, and arrangements in learning environments in the classroom and school to meet the needs of the CWDs.

Differentiation is a proactive intervention to assist CWDs in individualized learning and best meets the child's diverse needs. The focus is on the child's strengths and abilities, which allows individualization of subject content, learning process, and products to address the needs of the learner. Key factors in the design of teaching are a learner's readiness (individual needs, strengths, interests, preferences, and motivation), and previous experiences with the content, physical and psychological states, recent developmental stage, and specific academic aptitude. Differentiated instruction and multilevel lesson planning involve setting targets for learning outcomes in terms of academic (e.g., reading, writing, science, math) and functional skills, such as life skills in community. Differentiation involves the differentiation of learning content (e.g., what the child needs to learn); differentiation of process (how the child learns and the methods and pedagogies used); and differentiation of products (learning outcomes, knowledge and skills, and how are these presented and assessed).

Adequate learning materials, resources and tools, and teachers' effective use of these determine the quality of the child's learning. Inclusive education incorporates the utilization of information and communication technology, assistive technology devices, digital online learning materials, and software. These are effective when used by the teacher and child in a pedagogically sound way to achieve learning outcomes. Since CWDs are not a homogeneous group, different types of disability determine the required learning materials, resources, and support mechanisms in learning. Learners with physical disabilities may have a need of a completely different range of support mechanisms than those with mental disabilities, which need to be taken into account in the design of the inclusive education and learning environment.

A basic requirement is effortless access and a safe learning environment in inclusive education. Access to premises and facilities need to be secured, such as access to drinking water, playground, facilities, and spaces for extracurricular activities, music, dance, theater, art classes, vocational or technical rooms, restrooms and washrooms, school canteens, and laboratories.

Distinct safety and security guidelines are needed when including CWDs in mainstream education to prevent phsycial, mental, and sexual abuse, as well as exploitation of and discrimination against CWDs in the education premises and process. An important aspect is to have a policy of safe commuting to school with disability-friendly transportation and care providers in the transport to ensure safety and security of CWDs. Preventing sexual harassment, exploitation, and abuse needs to be an integral part of inclusive education policy. The vulnerability of CWDs needs to be duly considered in policy and program design for inclusive education. The safety and security measures must be factored in for both teachers and students. It is also critical to build self-awareness and knowledge among CWDs about bodily integrity and ensure their ability to inform concerned authorities and protect themselves.

Partnership is one of the key success factors in the development of inclusive education. At the national level, the government has the lead role in implementing inclusive education policy, legislation, and strategies, and in steering the actions in education institutions. In this regard, the governments and ministries need to work in partnerships with different stakeholders (donors, cross-ministerial, specialists, disability organizations, nongovernment organizations [NGOs]) to develop and implement inclusive education policy and practice for CWDs, e.g., in a sector-wide approach of education development.

At the school level, school directors, teachers, school boards, parent–teacher associations, and other school bodies have a role in the setting of school policies, rules, and practices for inclusive education. In communities, parents, health specialists and service providers, civil society organizations, NGOs, and other stakeholders working in partnership can greatly support CWDs in specific areas to ensure access to quality inclusive education.

In partnerships, all stakeholders (teachers, school directors, other education staff members, health specialists and service providers, NGOs, organizations for disabilities, parents of CWDs, individuals with disabilities, and others) have their specific roles and stake in the development of inclusive education to benefit CWDs. The guidance note emphasizes the collaboration and teamwork of all stakeholders to support the development of inclusive education for CWDs.

The field studies in the three DMCs revealed that all actors who have a stake in ensuring inclusive education to CWDs are well motivated to engage in partnerships to develop the education system and provide their support. The areas of cooperation and development include, for example, capacity building on the development of inclusive education systems for CWDs, teacher training for special education needs, inclusive classroom teaching and learning practices.

There is a strong need for capacity building and training of all stakeholders to make inclusive education a reality in mainstream education. Preservice and in-service teacher education, backed with academic research, are key to support teachers and make inclusive education and differentiated instruction a reality in the classroom. In addition, capacity building and training of all actors involved in the development of inclusive education, as well as awareness-raising of community members and society as a whole, are needed to pursue the common goal of inclusive education for CWDs.

International conventions and declarations, together with national laws and strategic planning on education of CWDs, provide a policy framework and steer the actions taken in education in DMCs. National governments take the lead in modernizing their education systems for inclusion of CWDs in education, effectively supported by development partners, civil society, academia, and other stakeholders in a sector-wide approach. The integration of CWDs in mainstream education policy and the provision of budget at par with other children are key issues.

Policymaking implies effective education data collection and an education management information system (EMIS) and setting targets for CWDs' inclusion. This requires data on access and enrollment in ECEC and basic education; out-of-school, retention, and gender-disaggregated data; graduation from basic and secondary levels; and transition to and graduation from TVET and higher education. Other targets for progress and data collection on CWDs in the EMIS may include the number of trained teachers, teachers with specialized training, number of support staff, sets of learning materials delivered, digital online learning materials, and schools with safe and flexible learning environments. The key factors for supporting the policies and practice of inclusive education with differentiated instruction are further elaborated in the following chapters of the guidance note.

I. INTRODUCTION

The technical assistance (TA) on Innovation in Education Sector Development in Asia and the Pacific by the Asian Development Bank (ADB) helped provide guidance on inclusive education with differentiated instruction. The TA helped to ensure that teaching is tailored to learners' levels in a manner that maximizes the benefit for children with disabilities (CWDs), and does not contribute to the stigmatization, exploitation, and abuse of any child.

CWDs suffer disproportionately from the learning crisis, further exacerbated by the coronavirus disease (COVID-19) pandemic. Although CWDs represent only around 5% of the total child population, they encompass more than half of out-of-school children globally (UNESCO 2018). There is a shared view in international education development that every child has the right to quality education. The recent development is toward promoting inclusive education where CWDs receive appropriate and high-quality education that is delivered alongside their peers. The global commitment to inclusive education is captured in the Sustainable Development Goal (SDG) 4—ensuring inclusive and equitable education and promoting lifelong learning opportunities for all.

In July 2018, ADB signed the Global Disability Summit Charter for Change, which was followed by a summit in February 2022. By signing the charter, ADB adopted several commitments to promote disability-inclusive development. The specific commitments of ADB to promote inclusive education include the following:

(i) Review of the education portfolio to identify the gaps and potential to more effectively support inclusion of the most marginalized children in society, including out-of-school girls and boys with disabilities.
(ii) Support for innovations to expand the quality, scope, and range of accessible materials and teaching approaches for learners with disabilities, and make their physical environment more accessible via universal design.

Since the COVID-19 pandemic, children have had widely differing access to quality education—with many receiving almost nothing for many months. The pandemic has highlighted the urgent need to shift teaching practices to ensure all children are learning. In the coming years, it will be more important than ever to tailor teaching to the level of all individual learners to ensure they have access to quality education that addresses their learning needs. It will be vital that inclusive education with differentiated and tailored instruction are rolled out in a fully inclusive way for all learners, including those with disabilities. Only by doing this shall children develop the foundational skills they need to become lifelong learners in line with the SDG 4.

This guidance note seeks to inform policy makers, practitioners, and other stakeholders on the importance of inclusive education and differentiated instruction for CWDs. The aim is to support the understanding of the opportunities and challenges of implementing inclusive education with differentiated instruction and to agree on the principles of education in a fully inclusive manner for the maximum benefit to CWDs. The project is carried out in cooperation with key stakeholders of policy makers, school leadership, teachers, civil society and advocacy organizations, persons with disability, and other key informants in the selected developing member countries (DMCs) of the Kyrgyz Republic, the Republic of the Marshall Islands, and Nepal.

II. METHODOLOGY

The methodology in preparing the guidance note included a literature review on the latest research findings as well as field interviews, focus group discussions (FGDs), and workshops in the selected DMCs. The approach has been to involve all relevant key stakeholders into participative inquiry and knowledge sharing based on predetermined questionnaires in each DMC. The key stakeholders in each of the DMCs have been agreed with the ADB resident missions in the respective countries.

The field data collected engaged key informants in face-to-face, online, and phone interviews; and FGDs involving stakeholders in the selected DMCs. The key stakeholder interviews included government officials, ADB staff, disability rights groups, nongovernment organizations (NGOs), and school leaders. The FGDs involved teachers, adults and students with disabilities, and parents of CWDs. There were around 50 persons engaged in the field inquiry.

The collected data were analyzed based on the key questions of the study focusing on the current legislation, statistics of school-aged CWDs, learning environments of CWDs, curricula development, teaching and learning, teachers' professional development on special education, collaboration of stakeholders, and other themes that emerged from the literature review and the field data. The guidance note presents the findings, conclusions, and recommendations to enhance the development of inclusive education with differentiated instruction for the learners with disabilities in ADB's DMCs.

Inclusive Education—A Global Definition

The global concept of inclusive education has evolved over the last 60 years. The United Nations Educational, Scientific and Cultural Organization (UNESCO) Convention Against Discrimination in Education (1960) interpretation prohibited "any exclusion from, or limitation to, educational opportunities on the basis of socially-ascribed or perceived differences, such as by gender, ethnic or social origin, language, religion, nationality, economic condition, ability," and focused generally on disability.

The Salamanca Statement (1994) expanded the concept from focusing only on children with special needs to children from all backgrounds: "All children should learn together, wherever possible, irrespective of any difficulties or differences they may have. Inclusive schools must recognize and respond to the diverse needs of their students." The Agenda for Sustainable Development for 2030 built on the Salamanca Statement in SDG 4 simplified the concept of inclusive education, emphasizing education for all and made a pledge to "leave no one behind." In the Cali Commitment (2019), countries joined to make preschools, schools, and other education settings as places where everyone is valued and belongs, and diversity is seen as enriching.

Education for all supports "the needs of the poor and the most disadvantaged, including working children; remote rural dwellers and nomads; ethnic and linguistic minorities; children, young people, and adults affected by conflict, HIV/AIDS, hunger, and poor health; and those with special learning needs." SDG 4.5 specifically reaffirms the need to "ensure equal access to all levels of education and vocational training for the vulnerable, including persons with disabilities, indigenous peoples, and children in vulnerable situations."

Today, the focus of inclusive education is vastly on how to support all children to learn successfully (Halinen and Järvinen 2008; Mitchell 2005). Inclusive education is understood as including all children regardless of gender, ethnic and linguistic minority or family background, disability or learning difficulty, or any other feature in mainstream education (UNESCO 2009). Inclusive education aims at increasing every learner's educational opportunities, in which teaching and learning processes are stimulated according to the learners' needs. There is a methodological shift from the traditional "one-size-fits-all" model toward individualized teaching and learning, which provides a starting point for educational equity (Lindner and Schwab 2020). Inclusion is further defined as "a transformative process that ensures full participation and access to quality learning opportunities for all children, young people, and adults, respecting and valuing diversity, and eliminating all forms of discrimination in and through education."

The concept of differentiated instruction recognizes and supports children as individual learners in their age-based peer group community. The differentiation practices view individuals, proactive intervention, and assisting individuals' educational needs and readiness as important to best meet student's diverse needs (Tomlinson 2000, 2003). Teachers in differentiated classrooms respect the level of each student's readiness. Readiness means the child's previous experiences with the content, physical and psychological states, recent developmental stage, and specific academic aptitude. In differentiated instruction, curricula design focuses not on student shortcomings but on their strengths and abilities, allowing individualization of subject content, learning process, and products for students within the curricula framework and targeted learning outcomes.

In a twin-tracked approach, there are overarching objectives in learning, which cover broad possibilities for fulfillment, such as developing competence in numeracy or literacy, which are the same for all students. However, the path to achieving them is different for each child, in which it is modified and offers several possibilities in consideration of content, extent, material, and instruction. What is respected in the individualized and adapted, inclusive pedagogy and teaching practices are the individual needs of students and individual students' learning pace.

Based on the student's needs, the learning content, extent, material, support, and assessment are tailored in the teaching. The methods and didactic approaches of differentiation and individualization are designed according to individual requirements to motivate all students to master individual tasks and achieve the learning outcomes. The concept and practice of the individual education plan (IEP) are adopted in many countries in education. For example, in the Kyrgyz Republic, the introduction of inclusive education and IEP is backed up by a 2-year program that aims to promote inclusive education and improve learning outcomes, supported by the United States Agency for International Development (USAID) and the United Nations Children's Fund (UNICEF).

The concept of inclusive education is to develop a comprehensive process that will allow every child, especially with special education needs, to have access to quality education in regular preschool and school with their peers.

Challenges in Implementing Inclusive Education at the Country Level

The persons involved in the study in the three countries understand and recognize the importance of inclusive education. Progress and challenges in implementing inclusive education were discussed during the interviews, FGDs, and workshops with the partners and stakeholders. The findings of the study reveal that the CWDs' learning environment highly depends on each country's educational policy and system. The learning environments of CWDs range from segregation to integration and inclusion. The main types of learning environments are as follows (Handicap International, Technical Resources Division 2012; Cali Commitment 2019):

(i) **Segregation.** Education for CWDs is offered, for example, at a special school or center. In a segregated learning environment, a child feels outside of the community and other children of the same age.
(ii) **Partial segregation.** This refers to an education system with both inclusion and segregation. Some CWDs receive education in mainstream schools, and others—usually children with severe disabilities—receive education in specialized schools.
(iii) **Integration.** CWDs learn in classes within a mainstream school, or CWDs are placed into mainstream classes, but without addressing specific learning or other critical needs. The learning of CWDs is not supported by modifying the curricula or teaching methods. A child learns in a separate environment, and are not encouraged to learn or mix together with other children.
(iv) **Inclusion.** All children are included in mainstream education. Quality education with differentiated instruction is offered to all children. Children of the same age cohort learn and play together. CWDs receive support services.

The field findings from the DMCs show that education for CWDs is still provided in segregated learning environments; in a special school; or in a center isolated from the community, from other children, and families. The discussions also revealed that, while integration classes (resources classes) for CWDs are placed in mainstream education, they do not receive sufficient support in specific learning or other critical needs. CWDs may be taught in separate classes for much or all of the time without proper learning arrangements or any possibility to mix and learn together with other children. CWDs in mainstream schools do not receive sufficient support in terms of modification of the curricula or adapting the teaching methods to the child's needs. Inclusion of CWDs in mainstream education requires proper development of the inclusive education system to avoid doing harm to the children.

The interviews noted that some parents refuse to send children with disabilities to school because of insufficient quality of teaching or accessibility and safety of the environment. The issues raised in the discussions were, for example, teachers' lack of competence in inclusive education, curricula that lacks adaptation, teaching and learning materials that are not accessible or adequate, infrastructures in and around schools that are not accessible, and lack of resources and measures to hinder bullying in overcrowded classes. In the three countries, while there are efforts toward inclusion, the governments have not yet succeeded in fully implementing inclusive education for CWDs in mainstream education.

In international development, data on disability in education are often limited as data collection and monitoring systems in the countries are insufficient (Mitra 2013). In particular, in low- and middle-income countries, there is a lack of disaggregated data on children and adults with disability, or the data are collected but not used. The lack of data (e.g., the type and degree of disability, gender, age, geographic location, and other factors) results in children being left out or being invisible in mainstream education. An appropriate data collection and monitoring mechanism is needed to reach out to the children concerned, understand exclusion experiences, provide inclusive education, and improve policy and planning for persons with disabilities.

There is also a lack of qualified teachers to implement inclusive education efficiently. This pertains not only to teachers' knowledge and skills in terms of inclusive practices, but also to the acceptance of inclusive values, which influence students' academic and behavioral performance at school (Savolainen et al. 2012). According to the interviewees, sufficient preservice or in-service teacher training and education in inclusive teaching that will benefit CWDs in mainstream education are not available in the three DMCs. In the United Kingdom, the in-service teacher education and training is a practice for continuing professional development. All schools have 5 days each year of in-service education and training. Schools are closed to pupils on these days, but staff attend. This type of education should be available for teachers and school staff on inclusive education.

III. GUIDANCE FOR INCLUSIVE EDUCATION

Commitment to International Declarations and Policies

A series of international legal and policy declarations and conventions support the right to free, quality, and inclusive education for all. These include the United Nations Convention on the Rights of Persons with Disabilities (UN CRPD) (2006), SDGs, Incheon Declaration, Oslo Declaration (2015), Global Disability Summit (2018), and the Cali Commitment (2019).

In the field inquiry, the UN CRPD was perceived as important, where Article 24 calls on State Parties to ensure inclusive education systems at all levels, and lifelong learning. Also, the SDG 4 goals are aimed to support progress in inclusive education for CWDs, as it commits to "ensure inclusive and equitable quality education and promote lifelong learning opportunities for all." The Cali Commitment (2019) highlights the need to accelerate the action, and to cooperate closely with civil society and marginalized groups. The international policies and legislation are effectively steering the rights of learners with disabilities to access inclusive and equitable quality education in mainstream education in parallel with their peers.

Many countries have signed the international policies and are committed to follow the legally binding or nonbinding conventions and principles in their national developments. The UN CRPD was ratified by Nepal in 2010, the Republic of Marshall Islands in 2015, and the Kyrgyz Republic in 2019. The countries signing the convention are committed to the rights of the persons with disabilities in their national legislation and policies.

Development of National Legislation and Policies

The UN Salamanca meeting (1994) called for the highest policy and budgetary priority to (i) improve inclusive education services; (ii) ensure inclusive education with legislation, and enroll all children in mainstream schools; (iii) ensure that organizations of persons with disabilities, parents, and communities are engaged in decision-making; (iv) develop preschool and vocational aspects of inclusive education; and (v) develop initial and in-service teacher education for teachers to have competence on inclusive education.

The field research of the DMCs reveals that, after almost 30 years, countries are still in the process of developing inclusive education for CWDs. As one interview of the study rightly noted, "the challenge is to connect the policies into practice." There is a need to improve policy steering and coordination to have an impact and improvement in inclusive teaching and learning in schools to benefit CWDs.

Over the past decades, education and training policies and systems in all countries have undergone fundamental reforms and changes. There has been a significant paradigm shift from the concept of "one-size-fits-all" to individualized and differentiated approaches in teaching and learning. Any revisions or updates in education laws or policies on inclusive education need to ensure not only the access to education, but also the quality and equity of education in terms of addressing the needs of individual learners, especially CWDs.

The recent trend in education development is to increase every learner's educational opportunities, where teaching and learning processes are stimulated to meet the students' diverse needs. In inclusive education, the methods and didactic approaches are designed according to individual requirements to motivate all children to achieve learning outcomes regardless of disability, learning difficulty, gender, or family background.

Governments' education policy development with a multidisciplinary approach encompasses coordination of work and cooperation of the ministries of education, health, and other sectors across the ministerial lines. The ministries need to ensure coordinated structures and systems for inclusive education and support services for CWDs. Local governments and schools need to follow the policy and develop a strategic action plan in terms of setting goals, deciding on actions to achieve those goals, and mobilizing the resources needed to take those actions for the inclusive education of CWDs. This should also include provision for external health and other services.

The European Union Eurydice Network provides European-level analyses and information on special education needs provision with mainstream education, geared for decision-makers responsible for education systems and policies in European countries (European Commission, Eurydice 2018). The online resources may also be helpful for DMCs to review the mainstream education and disability-specific policies, systems, and services; to identify gaps and barriers; and to plan actions to overcome them.

The national policymaking implies effective education data collection and education management information system (EMIS) and setting the targets for CWDs' inclusion—data on access and enrollment in early childhood education and care (ECEC) and basic education or those out of school, retention, gender-disaggregated data, graduation from basic and secondary levels, and transition to and graduation from technical and vocational education and training (TVET) and higher education.

Other targets for progress and data in the EMIS may include the number of trained teachers, number of teachers with specialized training, number of support staff, sets of learning materials delivered (including digital materials), and schools with safe and flexible learning environments. For example, the UNICEF Nepal Conference in December 2021 aimed to enhance the understanding of the situation of people and children living with disabilities in Nepal using existing data and evidence (UNICEF, Nepal 2021).

Utilization of a Twin-Tracked Approach

The needs of CWDs are the focus in the development of inclusive education (Handicap International - Humanity & Inclusion 2020). In inclusive education, a twin-tracked approach means that specialist support is provided for CWDs within mainstream education.

CWDs receive quality education as they are provided with additional and specific support targeted to their individual needs. The two-pronged strategy in inclusive education ensures that CWDs are on an equal basis with others in mainstream education. It also ensures that the specific needs of individual CWDs are targeted and addressed to empower them and enhance their learning. An individualized teaching and learning approach provides a starting point for inclusive education for CWDs.

The approach highlights the strengths and abilities of CWDs; whereas, the content, learning process, and products are individualized for CWDs. The content is what the child needs to learn; the process is the way the child arrives at the content; and the product refers to the child's understanding of the content. A child demonstrates the learning outcomes in terms of knowledge and skills.

Utilization of Differentiated Instruction

Children have had widely differing access to quality education because of the COVID-19 pandemic. Interviews conducted as part of the study reveal that learning supported by information and communication technology (ICT) has benefited most of those students who had good Internet connection and could afford computers and other technology and equipment at home. Children in rural areas or from families with low economic status were left out of education. Some countries developed TV and radio programs to reach students in the rural areas. Children in primary grades were also more affected. The pandemic has highlighted the urgent need to shift teaching practices to more flexible learning approaches to ensure all children, including CWDs, are learning.

Differentiated instruction recognizes and supports children as individual learners in their age-based peer group community. The differentiation practices view individuals, proactive intervention, and assisting individuals' educational needs and readiness as important to best meet students' diverse needs (Tomlinson 2003). Teachers in differentiated classrooms respect the level of each student's readiness, which is a result of many factors, such as their previous experiences with the content, physical and psychological states, recent developmental stage, and specific academic aptitude.

The Universal Design for Learning of CAST, Inc. highlights the following:
- **engagement** aims for purposeful, motivated learners, stimulating interest and motivation for learning;
- **representation** aims for resourceful, knowledgeable learners, and presents information and content in different ways; and
- **action and expression** aim for strategic, goal-directed learners and differentiated ways that students can express what they know.

Curriculum and instruction are differentiated using four primary methods: differentiation of content, process, product, and learning environment. These are elaborated in more detail in the ensuing paragraphs.

Differentiation of Content
Differentiation of content refers to the knowledge, understanding, and skills that students need to learn. While learning goals should remain the same for all students, in a differentiated classroom, what can be differentiated in terms of content is the method that students use to access key content. Scaffolding

content for CWDs may be used in all subject areas, allowing students the opportunity to master the skills within the range of their abilities.

For example, the differentiation of content may include the modification of the complexity in the area of study. The students can learn the same topic, but CWDs can have less complex information to learn the topic based on their abilities. Differentiating content also includes using various formats such as video, readings, lectures, audio, and similar formats according to the students' interests and abilities.

Differentiation of Process
Differentiation of process refers to how students understand and make sense of the content. The learning process needs to be differentiated according to different types of disabilities. For example, curricula are often too dependent on text form. Therefore, alternative ways in the learning process utilize different sensory avenues. The process has different levels of difficulty and options for different interests of learners. Activities that are collaborative-based—as opposed to those performed strictly individually—are examples of differentiating the process.

Differentiation of Product
Differentiation of product is the demonstration of how students have come to understand the content. Allowing children with different types of disabilities to demonstrate their learning in a way that emphasizes their accomplishments is important. CWDs may choose to utilize technology or drawing and illustrations to show their learning instead of giving oral presentations.

Differentiation of the Learning Environment
Differentiation of the learning environment refers to the modification of the learning environment to meet students' emotional and physical safety needs. Having a flexible learning space where learners can learn and grow is important not only for CWDs, but for all children. The flexible learning space may incorporate elements, such as quiet corners, lap or standing desks, and comfortable seating, among others. The learning environment must ensure the safety and security of children from disaster, accidents, abuse, and exploitation.

Screening and Identification Programs

Early detection of developmental delays and impairments is as crucial as a child's first 3 years of life. CWDs are often not diagnosed or are misdiagnosed due to the lack of disability screening and identification programs.

When children do not reach milestones by a certain age, these are warning signs that should not be ignored. Children may need extra support and services. To address the need for internationally comparable information about the frequency and situation of CWDs, UNICEF has recommended that countries screen for disability in the Multiple Indicator Cluster Survey program as part of household surveys (Brossard 2021).

However, household surveys are not conducted each year. Therefore, staff in children's hospitals and education systems need to be available to identify disability in children. The staff can refer the children for proper screening for identification of CWDs by specialized professionals with rigorous training in the assessment. The proper screening entails the use of a standardized method of assessment for disability type, degree, and categorization. The screening and identification need to have parental consent and the consent of the person with disability, when possible.

The field study reveals that screening of CWDs is an area that needs development in the countries studied. There have been early attempts to use screening methods—e.g., the Washington set of questions (Washington Group on Disability Statistics) to focus on proper screening and identification. However, knowledge and capacity by schools and health professionals to undertake professional screening for the purpose of inclusive education are rather insufficient.

Screening at early childhood is especially important to develop support for inclusion in education. According to the interviews, teachers are not able to screen and identify CWDs. Children who are identified are often misidentified for their disability—e.g., a hearing impaired child may be identified as intellectually impaired. The interviews note that it is difficult to design plans and programs when the resources and capacity to screen and identify CWDs are not available.

In Nepal, a pilot project on screening, funded by World Education and UNICEF, was conducted in 2017 by Humanity and Inclusion. Children with ages of 4-7 years were assessed regarding functional limitations. The pilot revealed that 26% of children had a risk of at least some kind of limitation (hearing, sight, mobility, communication, learning, concentration). In the pilot, 9.4% of the children were classified as having a disability (Handicap International - Humanity & Inclusion 2018).

Compulsory Inclusive Education in Early Childhood Education and Care Programs

Screening is especially important to ensure access to inclusive ECEC for CWDs. Approximately 90% of a child's brain is formed prior to the age of 6. Interviews in the study reveal a consensus that CWDs should enter inclusive education at the level of ECEC. However, the field study reveals that, currently, there is insufficient knowledge and capacity to competently undertake screening by multiprofessional teams involving education, health, and other authorities relevant to the promotion of access of CWDs to inclusive education. As the interviews note, it is difficult to design education plans and programs for CWDs when the resources and capacities are not available in schools.

Most CWDs in developing countries are not enrolled in ECEC. According to a UNICEF report, among the important factors determining the child's enrollment in pre-primary education are the child's household wealth, mother's education level, and geographical location (UNICEF Data 2019). However, poverty is the single largest determining factor for exclusion in ECEC. The discussions with the interviewees noted that disability-friendly private ECEC is available with quality learning for CWDs, but poor families cannot afford them.

Quality learning in early childhood sets a strong foundation for CWDs to start learning and advance to the next levels of achievements in inclusive education. There is a need for improved inclusive public ECEC provision for CWDs. Quality-inclusive early learning provides CWDs with multiple ways to activate learning with materials and toys. It provides children with different ways to express what they know, making individualized modifications to support a child's learning, providing opportunities for children to interact and work together, and supporting or guiding a child as they learn or acquire a new skill.

Capacity Building on Inclusive Education

The role of teachers is crucial in implementing inclusive education efficiently (Forlin et al. 2010). It is evidenced that not only teachers' knowledge and skills on inclusive practices, but also their acceptance of inclusive values, influence students' academic and behavioral performance at school (Savolainen et al. 2012). Teachers who have more contact and experience with CWDs and have training on inclusive education hold more positive attitudes toward inclusive education (Malinen, Savolainen, and Xu 2012). Therefore, capacity building and training are needed for teachers, with both theoretical knowledge and opportunities for teaching in practice to test the aptitude to become a good inclusive educator.

Inclusive Education as Focus Area in Capacity Building and Teacher Education

The field inquiry reveals that there is a shortage of teachers to support learning of CWDs in the DMCs studied. The lack of professional teachers is one of the key factors for schools not accepting CWDs or for parents not sending their child to school. In inclusive education, self-efficacy of teachers is important.

The term "self-efficacy" can be defined as one's belief in one's abilities to perform effectively under certain situations (Klassen et al. 2011). It has been demonstrated that teachers' self-efficacy promotes positive attitudes toward inclusive education (Malinen, Savolainen, and Xu 2012; Savolainen et al. 2012; Sharma et al. 2018). Therefore, it is important that all teachers are trained (in preservice and in-service teacher training) on inclusion of CWDs in mainstream education. Teacher training should include courses and modules focused on the pedagogy and instruction of CWDs to address the needs of diverse student populations in mainstream education.

In inclusive education, the role of special education teachers is essential. The interviews in the three DMCs show that universities may play a central role in supporting teacher education for special education teachers. Furthermore, research on special education needs can effectively expand the knowledge on inclusive education at all levels. The provision of university-level special education programs and diploma courses for teachers specializing on special education needs is seen as one way to improve the quality and professionalism of inclusive teaching for CWDs in schools. Teacher programs for special education teachers should also include teaching practice to assess the teachers' aptitude to the teaching profession for CWDs.

Online teacher training modules, which provide training on inclusive education have become popular among teachers due to its flexibility, in particular during the COVID-19 situation. The interviews reveal that, as a result of the different types of capacity building (formal and nonformal), communities of practice of educators are emerging in social media to share and conduct peer-learning on inclusive education for CWDs, such as those in Nepal and the Kyrgyz Republic. The interviews note that ministries should acknowledge and provide incentives for teachers to take up training on inclusive education provided by civil society organizations and add certification to their credentials.

In inclusive education, the general education teachers and special education teachers work together and in teams to support CWDs. These teachers also need to work with other professionals, such as psychologists, nurses, social workers, assistants, counselors, therapists, and those who work in and with schools. The field inquiry reveals that the services provided for CWDs by the professionals vary greatly at the national, municipal, and school levels in the DMCs. For example, the interviewees noted that

CWDs in rural areas are excluded from many services that are available in the capital and urban areas. It is widely acknowledged that multiprofessional collaboration in teaching and learning has high potential to support student learning in inclusive classrooms (Björn et al. 2016).

In-Service Training Focused on Inclusive Education for All Educators

Positive attitude and self-efficacy of all staff are important when including CWDs in a school environment and in mainstream education. All education staff, including decision-makers, technical staff, service providers, and others who work in schools, need to have positive attitudes toward inclusive education. All staff need to be trained on how to handle, motivate, teach, and manage CWDs as they are all responsible for the safety and security of CWDs.

Research shows that local education authorities, school principals, and school management groups have a crucial role in developing inclusive education into actual practices (Vainikainen et al. 2015). In schools with inclusive culture, teachers and school staff share the same outlook regarding respect for diversity and a commitment to providing learning opportunities to all children. Noting the importance of the school leadership to promote inclusive education, capacity building on inclusive education is needed for local education authorities, school principals, and local school management groups. Inclusive education needs to become part of the government's institutional capacity building and training of education officers. This training can be part of the organizations' personnel training. Disability organizations, NGOs, and development partners may also provide projects with pilots of inclusive education.

The field data finding is that international and national NGOs and civil society organizations in DMCs support inclusive education with different education and capacity-building programs. Many of them provide nonformal training programs on inclusive education and support teachers' continued professional development on teaching CWDs, but are limited to specific regions or specialization areas.

For example, in Nepal, Humanity and Inclusion, funded by USAID Nepal, is implementing a reading project that supports thousands of Nepali CWDs to achieve better reading outcomes. The project develops methods of instruction to benefit CWDs. It provides training for professionals of teaching and curriculum development to have skills to use the "Reading for All" tools and promote inclusive education in Nepal (Handicap International - Humanity & Inclusion 2018). In addition to supporting the identification and enrollment of CWDs in 10 schools and 10 preschools in the same communities, the pilot initiative will introduce multilingual education in 20 schools to improve reading outcomes of children. The most successful tools and approaches will be replicated and used to inform nationwide work on inclusive education (UNICEF, Kyrgystan 2018).

Ensuring Safety and Security of Learning Environments

One of the reasons for CWDs being out of school is the lack of a safe or disability-friendly learning environment. Most schools and learning environments are designed and maintained for able-bodied student populations. The interviews reveal that some schools have inaccessible infrastructures in and around schools. For example, children with physical disabilities frequently have trouble accessing hygiene facilities. Moreover, there are insufficient measures to hinder bullying of CWDs in classes.

Safety of learning environments should consider not just physical safety and security in terms of access and accidents, but also safety from harassment, abuse, exploitation, and discrimination. The safety and security of CWDS should be ensured, covering the whole school environment—e.g., restrooms, washrooms, playground area, accessible drinking water, lunch meals, and locks that are reachable and friendly for CWDs. It is likewise important that support staff are available to help CWDs in using such facilities.

Regarding specific needs of CWDs, classrooms that are not well-lit are not conducive for learners with visual disabilities. Children with mental disabilities often require a quiet or calm space. School yards are not well maintained for CWDs with physical disabilites. The interviews note that some schools have taken active measures to ensure safe and comfortable learning environments for CWDs. For example, one school has secured a quiet room for CWDs to take a rest during the school day. School principals and school boards have a key position in fostering a safe and secure inclusive learning environment for CWDs.

Distinct safety and security guidelines are needed when including CWDs in mainstream education to prevent physical, mental, and sexual abuse, as well as exploitation and discrimination of CWDs in the education premises and process. An important aspect is to have a policy of safe commuting to school with disability-friendly transportation and care provider in the transport to ensure safety and security of CWDs.

Disability-Friendly Curriculum and Resources

The need for multilevel lesson planning that is manageable in a standards-based instructional context, along with a variety of instructional strategies, is widely acknowledged (Lawrence-Brown 2004). Planning starts from national or core curriculum and is differentiated into adapted or prioritized curriculum for learners with disabilities. The curriculum may be customized for certain types or categories of disability or by level that a child is attending. Schools can customize the curriculum according to the local resources in decentralized education systems.

Adapted or Prioritized Curriculum

Curriculum in general education schools is often designed as a one-size-fits-all model, without taking into consideration the specific needs of CWDs. Current education policies indicate the need to review and revise the curriculum to ensure that CWDs can fully participate in mainstream education. None of the countries in this study have reported introducing adapted curricula by the government. However, it is likely that there are adaptations initiated by schools in integrated or resource classes.

According to UNICEF, curricular reform is an essential strategy for educational change (Brossard 2021; UNICEF 2021), whereby the educational aims, content areas, learning outcomes, and assessment systems are reviewed and restructured. The learning materials, and teaching and learning methodologies are upgraded accordingly. For example, in Bhutan, a recent participative consultation with stakeholders led to the drafting of a resolution for the development of a diversified and differentiated curriculum in 2020 (Drukpa 2020). The prioritized and adapted curriculum comprises about 35%–40% of the actual school curricula and is modified from the prescribed program of studies to meet the learning requirements of students, with emphasis on numeracy, literacy, and life skills delivered in themes and key stages.

Similarly, a prioritized curriculum is carefully selected from learning experiences. This is grade-specific and subject-specific, which each student must know and accomplish by the end of each school year for the standards of the next grade. It comprises 65% of the normal or regular learning content. The prioritized curriculum in Bhutan emphasizes the development of understanding and competencies on fundamental concepts and ideas in the subjects. The learning outcomes are defined by a set of standards or results, in terms of procedural knowledge, skills, strategies, and processes. The curricular reforms and innovations in DMCs may provide opportunities for improved inclusion of CWDs in mainstream education.

Curriculum needs to be adapted and differentiated to meet the vast range of types and degrees of disabilities that may be present in a classroom. There are several factors to consider in adapting the curriculum—assessing the content of learning and goals for learning outcomes, reflecting the teaching strategies, flexible scheduling, instruction in large or small groups, complementing the learning with individualized instruction or tutorials, and cooperative learning with peers. The curriculum adaptation reviews the form of instruction to meet the individual needs of children with special needs, as well as the delivery and response factors that the child will receive in school.

Other factors can also be considered in the curriculum planning (e.g., rural, urban, poor, low income, middle income, high income, ethnic group, native language, among others) as these affect a child's cognitive process through early socialization process and norms that may impact how a child is able to perform and adjust to his or her learning environment.

A key to success in an inclusive classroom is to have adaptation, accommodation, and modification made to the teaching and learning activities according to the needs of each child with disabilities (Center for Parent Information and Resources 2020). Teaching and learning is adapted to address the needs of a child, considering the type and degree of disability. When adapting instruction to the child's needs, it considers what a child learns and how at school. Modification or accommodation in the classroom includes, among others,

- scheduling the time for learning (e.g., extra time to do assignments or tests);
- organizing the learning setting (e.g., small group or individually with the teacher);
- offering a variety of learning materials (e.g., Braille audio lectures, books, videos, games);
- differentiated instruction (e.g., reducing the level of difficulty and scope of tasks, extra support by a student or peer); and
- allowing diversity in students' responses (e.g., allowing answers to be given orally or dictated, using a word processor for written work, using sign language or a communication device, drawing a picture).

Adapted Curriculum for Technical, Vocational, and Higher Education

Inclusive education in technical and vocational education and training (TVET) is intended for students who need special support with their studies and/or work-based learning. The need for special education may arise from the student's disability, learning difficulties, mental or physical health problems, or social difficulties.

Curricula and programs that support students with disabilities in TVET include upper secondary vocational qualifications, preparatory education for upper secondary vocational studies, and preparatory education for work and independent living. Teaching and learning for students with disabilities is usually organized in small groups. Students are also provided with individual guidance and support in their studies, as well as progress to employment and daily living. Some TVET schools organize or arrange a period for learners with disability to test their aptitude, interest, and abilities in different TVET fields. The experiment period may also involve assessing the need for support services relating to teaching, learning, and daily living. The curricula should be adapted accordingly to meet the individual needs of the students.

In TVET, each student with disability needs an individual education plan (IEP). The IEP is revised throughout the period of study, and it involves an assessment and a follow-up plan. The focus of the plan is on practical rather than theoretical learning, with the aim of achieving skills in specific occupational fields. Students with disability in TVET need individual support and well-being services in issues relating to studies, rehabilitation, and employment. Gender considerations and safety and security measures should be ensured, especially for CWDs who are girls or from marginalized groups in residential trainings. Cooperation with the students, their families, and other experts forms an integral part of the studies. Often, the TVET schools offer accommodation with related support services for students with disability to facilitate independent living. TVET institutions may also function as development centers of special needs education and training, offering in-service training and consultancy and producing materials for special needs learners in TVET.

Implementing inclusive education in higher education is an area that needs further development. Inclusive education has been first developed for younger students before higher education. The clamor for inclusive practices within higher education has intensified over the past few years, since more and more students with disabilities graduate from secondary education (Moriña 2017). Research shows that lecturer attitudes, practices in the classroom, curricular adaptations, and faculty training play key roles in improving inclusion in higher education. Higher education institutions need to have strategies and actions both at the institutional level and in the classroom setting to ensure inclusion of students with disabilities.

As in all education, university environments need to be fully accessible without any physical barriers. The needs of students with disabilities have to be taken into account in teaching strategies and methods of higher education. Support strategies include, for example, orientation sessions, tutorials, and persons or groups who support students with disability in the faculty. Faculty members should be informed and trained on inclusive pedagogy and universal designs for learning. Inclusive higher education guarantees that all the students participate fully and benefit from a process of quality teaching and learning. For example, in the Kyrgyz Republic, a government decree was adopted in 2019 ensuring that learners with disabilities can study at universities.

Utilization of Multilevel Lesson Planning
Adapted or prioritized curriculum usually includes objectives for both academic and functional skills. Adapted curriculum may include content of general curriculum, but also functional and life skills. Priorities are determined by the needs of an individual student (specific strengths, needs, interests, and preferences). Individual and person-centered planning will determine the priorities.

An example of authentic instruction is learning functional skills in a botanical garden. A classroom in mainstream school, equipped with needed adaptations, can serve as the most integrated and inclusive environment for learning most IEP goals for CWDs. In addition, community-based instruction for persons with disabilities may support functional skills and free-time activities, as well as promote in-school-to-work transition (Lawrence-Brown 2004). In the design of the adapted curricula for CWDs, the environment-related variables refer to physical support such as materials for teaching, resources, assistive technology tools (Braille), and ICT equipment; human support (e.g., teacher assistants, special education teachers, professionals external to the school); and the community context. Instruction in local spoken dialect can facilitate the integration of CWDs in school and education environment.

An IEP needs to be compulsory for all children with disabilities in inclusive education. The plan should include learning purpose, learning objectives, topic areas, methods to learn them, timetable, methods of assessing the learning outcomes, analysis of strengths and weaknesses, feedback, and means for setting new learning objectives. Based on the IEP and the learning outcomes, CWDs can compile a portfolio of their learning outputs or products. Didactic approaches depend on individual requirements. Differentiation and individualization aim to motivate all students to master individual tasks and achieve learning outcomes.

The background of CWD students can inform teachers about the risks and opportunities for each child in terms of access to and retention education. A child's ability to continue his or her education depends on a number of factors. Children may be taken out of schools because of, for example, poverty. CWDs may also drop out of school to help in household or farm chores. It is good to have a system to identify risk factors and opportunities that may exclude the child from education.

Utilization of Information and Communication Technology and Assistive Technology Devices

The World Health Organization (WHO) has provided a Priority Assistive Products List (WHO 2016), which is useful for basic assistive products. The list is not specific to inclusive education for CWDs, but may provide a model for listing priority assistive products for needs of specific disabilities in schools. Assistive technology may range from low- to high-technology devices. For example, augmentative and alternative communication devices are developed to support people who have disorder in communication. These devices can range from a simple picture board to a computer program that synthesizes speech from text.

There are many opportunities to use assistive technology and devices to support learning of CWDs. The aim with the technology and devices is to support learning where tasks are challenging, such as handwriting. Assistive technology needs to be complementary to teaching and instruction. Teachers should be trained to have the capacity to integrate assistive technology into teaching and learning in a meaningful way so that the devices do not pose a distraction from learning. The interviews suggest that it is important to invest in basic assistive products and that teachers need the competence to use the assistive devices in a pedagogically sound way to support the learning of CWDs.

ICT has the ability to transform and open up education and learning also to persons with disabilities (UNESCO 2013). Websites, mobile devices and services, TV, radio, and other emerging technologies can contribute to access and inclusion in education. Mobile devices are portable and easy to carry. For CWDs, a mobile device enables access to learning at the time of need and from anywhere with connectivity. However, CWDs from the most vulnerable households may not have access to smartphones, which are required for ICT-based learning. For example, most students in Nepal could not access ICT-based education because of lack of access to devices or lack of connectivity during the COVID-19 restrictions. Instead, distance education was provided via TV and radio broadcasts. Therefore, the government needs to invest in ICT devices and network infrastructure in inclusive schools with CWDs.

In India, the Pratham Open Basic Education program develops designed solutions to include children who are unable to cope with mainstream education curriculum and assessment. Digital resources are developed on Indian Sign Language and Activities of Daily Living and aim to support schools, communities, and parents in the care and learning of CWDs. For example, online digital assessment tools have been developed to assess the learning outcomes, which are incorporated digitally into the formal national assessment system for children in homeschooling. Digital training and guidance for parents, and learning materials and tools have been developed that connect learners with disabilities into mainstream education system, and these are available on the market.

Mobile devices and services can support students with disabilities in living independently outside their homes. The student can get on-demand support for independent living via SMS, voice calls, or through other means. The student can communicate with emergency services, family members, personal aides, and assistive services through mobile devices. Free broadband is a prerequisite to have access to inclusive communication and learning networks. The government needs to invest on technology to support students with disabilities—i.e., not only to aid in their learning process but also to help them lead an independent life.

Provision of Support Services for Families of Children with Disabilities

Parent Support and Education Programs
The interviews conducted for this study note that all parents would like to get education for CWDs. However, parents have concerns about accessibility, quality of teaching and learning, safety, transportation, etc. Interviewed parents of CWDs expressed the need for protection of their children and are concerned with the vulnerability of their children in school. Parents have the right to decide about the education of their children.

Governments should advocate the rights of parents and ensure that CWDs have access to quality and safe inclusive education, complemented with support services. The education service needs to work in close cooperation with parents and families of CWDs in their local communities. Parents who were interviewed expressed willingness to give their support in ensuring inclusive education for CWDs. In one case, a parent had even established a school, as she could not find a safe and quality learning environment for her child. Therefore, the education service, in consultation with parents, needs to develop specific safety and security policy and protocol for CWDs in school and learning environments, transport, and the use of various facilities in the school premises.

Creation of a Referral Pathway for Services

Families of CWDs often do not know who to reach out to when they are in need of support services; therefore, the responsibility often falls on the school and health administrators who are responsible for the availability of the support services. The referral pathway should ideally begin before a child is even identified as having a developmental delay or disability and, at the onset, should include community education programs for parents on the warning signs of developmental delays and clear guidance on how to pursue and secure screening. This could include materials and resources at a health provider's office, given out during mobile clinics or shared during parenting groups.

Children from poor families have even more barriers to attending school than children from non-economically disadvantaged families. Therefore, the referral pathway should include financial and well-being support programs for CWDs and their families, with education offering scholarship opportunities for CWDs so they are able to pursue TVET, university, or other higher education programs. The interviews reveal that the countries studied have financial support and social service systems. However, the interviewees note that financial support is minimal. It is therefore recommended that governments design a referral pathway for inclusion to social services and protection, and inform schools and local authorities about it.

For example, in Nepal, a project by the Himalayan Education and Development (HEAD Nepal) developed advisory and counseling services to persons with disabilities and their networks. The project aims to provide information and advice to persons with disabilities, their families, friends, colleagues, caregivers, service providers, and the public. The support service covers family counseling and encouraging persons with disabilities themselves to find information, including finding the right services, support, and advocacy groups and other community information related to specific disabilities.

Encouragement of Partnership Approaches

A multidisciplinary approach is the basis to provide inclusive education suited to the needs of CWDs. In inclusive education, the right assessment of the needs of CWDs requires a multidisciplinary approach. In multidisciplinary teams, experts from different disciplines are in a good position to work together to define the challenges and find solutions for the benefit of CWDs.

Involvement and Cooperation

The interviews and focus group discussions (FGDs) show that children and adults with disabilities and their parents are well motivated to engage in the development of inclusive education in the DMCs. Some of the persons with disabilities who were interviewed have graduated and are actively working in organizations to improve the education of CWDs in their countries, such as in the Kyrgyz Republic. The countries should not have any policy development regarding inclusive education without listening to the views of the persons with disabilities. In inclusive education, it is important to involve persons and learners with disabilities to more effectively adjust the teaching and learning to their needs. It would also be beneficial to recruit and prioritize teachers belonging to groups of persons with disabilities.

Teacher, Support Personnel, and Provider Partnerships

Inclusive practices in teaching highlight collaboration and teamwork to improve instructional and organizational practices. In collaboration and co-teaching, all teaching personnel support the students. Teachers should cooperate with other professionals (e.g., special education teachers, speech and physiotherapists, psychologists), and with family members and students themselves. A multidisciplinary approach ensures providing services to meet the specific needs of CWDs. In inclusive education, it involves assembling experts from other fields other than special education to form multidisciplinary teams to help teachers and special education teachers in the delivery of education and other services to CWDs. The focus should be on CWDs and the solutions to include them in quality education and learning in mainstream education.

Government and Organizational Partnerships

Several approaches and strategies can be identified to educate CWDs in mainstream education. Governments can benefit from strong collaboration, and working in partnership, with key stakeholders. These include civil society organizations and donors, which are crucial in improving the quality of teaching and learning for CWDs, such as in Nepal's sector-wide education development. Organizations of persons with disabilities, as well as parents and other stakeholders, are key advocates to improving the quality of education provision for CWDs. These organizations are also key service providers for persons with disabilities, helping fill the gaps in public education provision. One of the partnership approaches that can strongly contribute to the quality of inclusive public education for CWDs is collaboration with national and international civil society organizations and NGOs.

For example, the Government of Nepal, with strong NGO partners including USAID Nepal, World Education, Nepal Association for the Welfare of the Blind, National Federation of the Deaf Nepal, and Disable Empowerment and Communication Center, together with other local actors, is implementing the Reading for All project set up to support Nepali CWDs. The project has included 2,071 schools in four districts. It involves training head teachers for leading early detection and screenings (178,117 children through Grade 3). The project aims to continue in other districts to reach 557,828 students (Handicap International - Humanity & Inclusion 2018).

Many countries have moved to decentralized decision-making in education, and spending is delegated to subnational levels—e.g., local governance in Nepal. The governments need cooperation and coordination between central and local authorities to deliver quality education services. Effective, well-coordinated decentralization strategies have the potential to improve the quality of education services for CWDs and to use education resources more efficiently.

Collecting disaggregated data on disability is a priority for effective inclusive education strategies and frameworks. Disability disaggregated data should include retention rate and/or continuity of education and achievement of learning outcomes, in addition to enrollment rates and number of students. The data should be disaggregated by gender and ethnicity to enable a proper analysis if inclusive education is equally benefiting all CWDs, including those from the most marginalized groups.

Universities and research organizations are important partners in improving research and teacher education on CWDs. Even one faculty member in a university can greatly help special needs education by supporting quality teacher programs and qualified teaching staff in schools.

Designing an Inclusive Education Project

ADB is committed to promote disability-inclusive development and innovations in education to expand the quality, scope, and range of accessible materials and teaching approaches for learners with disabilities, and to make their physical environment more accessible via universal design. The following guidance aims to support the design of inclusive projects in education by ADB in DMCs.

- **International declarations and national policies.** Review the country's existing policy framework and commitment to international declarations and the existing national legislation. Assess the feasibility of the project within the current policy framework and operational environment; review the need for any revisions for the purpose of the project.
- **Sector-wide approach.** Adopt a sector-wide holistic approach in inclusive education development, where the government and relevant ministries work together with beneficiaries, stakeholders, and donors to coordinate resources and actions toward a common objective.
- **Reforms to inclusive education.** Introduce reforms and changes for inclusive education in both education policy and practice. Ensure that the project has education policy and strategy implications, which benefit CWDs in practice at school level. Introduce changes that have an impact on all levels of education, e.g., transition and retainment of CWDs in education. Initiate changes in the education system with sustainable and long-term effects.
- **Multidisciplinary approach and piloting.** Engage partners comprising cross-sector and multiprofessional teams to develop the project and its activities. Test project in an authentic school environment involving CWDs and gather feedback from key beneficiaries for improvements.
- **Participate, engage, and consult.** Actively engage and consult with families, as well as organizations, of CWDs on an equal basis as they are the beneficiaries of the project's outcomes. Engage organizations, such as NGOs, who already have experience of working in the area of development to build on lessons learned.
- **Innovation.** Introduce innovation to inclusive education with a twin-tracked approach. Introduce international good practices (e.g., Universal Design of Learning Guidelines), digitalization, and others that are currently driving innovation in inclusive education development.
- **Needs analysis.** Prepare the project based on strong needs analysis and field inquiry involving a wide representation of stakeholders on disability. Focus on key beneficiaries of learners with disabilities and their needs in the analysis. Justify the needs with an appraisal based on evidence of studies and interviews.
- **Define the area of intervention.** Define and delimit the area of development to a specific population, geographical area, etc. At the same time, plan the scalability to the whole education system and targeted population. Consider not only the reform of teaching and learning of CWDs in the school, but also the whole-life environment of persons with disabilities (learning environment within the school and premises, transportation to school, learning at home online, medical care, free-time and social activities in the community, etc.).
- **Define the targeted group.** Define the targeted group and analyze the needs of the learners with disabilities thoroughly to succeed and have an impact with the project. Define the ecosystem of inclusive education in terms of what are the institutions and/or who are the staff and persons supporting these learners with disabilities, and what capacities do they need.
- **Data system.** Develop the education management information system (EMIS) for the purpose of inclusive education. Set clear qualitative and quantitative indicators for the project in EMIS. Use the data system to monitor progress, assess success, and make improvements regularly.

- **Activities.** Focus on a child or student with disability in the project's activities. There are many stakeholders who have their diverse interests in the development. It is important to keep the focus on activities to change and improve the education of learners with disabilities for inclusion in mainstream education.
- **Monitor and evaluate.** Collect feedback from the key beneficiaries throughout the project. Make revisions accordingly and improve the quality of the project's outcomes.
- **Results and deliverables.** Ensure that the results and deliverables of the project benefit the child and student with disability, with inclusive education and differentiated approaches in teaching and learning with long-term effects.
- **Piloting and scaling.** After the piloting, multiply and scale up the project's outcomes in a wider scope of locations and populations for impact and sustainability.
- **Invest in advocacy and visibility.** Promote inclusion of learners with disabilities in mainstream education in the project. Inform and advocate the wider stakeholders, decision-makers, authorities, and communities about the intervention and innovation.

IV. CONCLUSIONS AND RECOMMENDATIONS

Conclusions

The key conclusion of the study is that every child—including children with disabilities (CWDs)—has a right to quality inclusive education. The aim of this guidance note drawn from research and discussions with stakeholders in the three DMCs is to support policy makers and practitioners in DMCs to make inclusive education with differentiated instruction a reality to benefit CWDs.

For Governments

- **Partnerships in sector-wide approach for inclusion.** The study concludes that collaboration and multistakeholder partnerships are needed to develop inclusive education. A good practice is a whole-system approach (sector-wide approach), where the government and/or ministry of education, together with donors and other stakeholders, can coordinate resources and actions in inclusive education, and initiate and steer changes benefiting CWDs at school level.
- **Disability-disaggregated data.** Data on CWDs are needed for proper analysis of the situation of CWDs regarding inclusion in mainstream education. Data with multiple dimensions on inclusive education can be collected, e.g., in EMIS on access, enrollment, retention, levels, transition, and graduation, along with the number of trained teachers, support staff, sets of learning materials available, learning outcomes, schools with safe and flexible learning environments, among others.
- **Monitoring and evaluation.** A system on inclusive education that specifically targets CWDs is needed to monitor progress and set clear targets and indicators to follow up regularly.
- **Financial and human resources.** Resources need to be budgeted to implement disability-friendly and inclusive education that specifically targets CWDs.
- **Partnerships and collaboration.** In inclusive education, targeting CWDs incorporates cooperation of specialists from different areas. The government benefits from the specific expertise of all stakeholders and works in partnership to support inclusive education, including with civil society organizations, disability organizations, parents' associations, education specialists and researchers, medical specialists, and therapeutic and other support service providers.
- **Curricula.** Curricula are reformed where a one-size-fits-all model is replaced with adapted or prioritized curricula and individual education plans (IEPs), allowing differentiation of subject context, learning process, and products to the needs of learners with disabilities.
- **Twin-tracked approach.** Inclusion is promoted in mainstream education while, at the same time, special support is provided for learners with disabilities.
- **Early childhood learning and care.** Inclusion of CWDs into mainstream education should start in early childhood education and care (ECEC) programs to ensure a successful base in learning and progression from one education level to the next.
- **Transition.** Inclusive education includes support for the learner with disability to progress from one level to another (basic, TVET, higher education). The progress is supported with special measures.

- **Screening.** Early screening and an assessment are done by a team of professionals (specialists from health, education, and social fields) who can make recommendations for successful inclusion of CWDs into education and full participation in society in later life.
- **Referral system.** A referral system is important for families with CWDs. A referral system needs to be available for families and parents for advice on rights, services, materials and resources, free-time activities, organizations providing support, among others.
- **International conventions and declarations.** Government policies may need to be updated to stay aligned with international policy development regarding inclusive education. There is a need for continued development and updating of national legislation and policies accordingly.

For Schools

- **Commitment to inclusive education.** Schools at all levels, from ECEC to higher education in the whole educational environment, need to be committed to implementing inclusive education into their school strategies and practices in teaching and learning.
- **Capacity building and training.** All education staff (teachers and school staff, members of school bodies, school administration) need capacity building and training to commit to inclusive education as a core value.
- **Teacher training.** Competence and self-efficacy of teachers are needed to embed inclusive education into the practices of teaching and learning. Preservice and in-service teacher trainings are needed for inclusiveness. Teacher trainings should also include prioritization of special education teachers who are specifically trained for CWD education, including different types of disabilities.
- **Individual education plan.** An IEP is a requirement for inclusion of CWDs in mainstream education. It is designed according to an adapted curriculum with learning objectives, areas of learning, methods, timetable, assessment methods, recognition of learning outcomes in terms of knowledge and skills, and feedback.
- **Inclusive learning environment.** A safe, secure, functional, and disability-friendly learning environment is a prerequisite of inclusive education. Accessibility within and outside the school building and safe transportation should be ensured. Distinct safety and security guidelines are needed when including CWDs in mainstream education to prevent phsycial, mental and sexual abuse, and exploitation and discrimination.
- **Differentiated instruction.** Differentiation includes adopting proactive intervention in the classroom with multilevel lesson planning; differentiating the content, process, and product of learning; taking into consideration the readiness, interest strength, motivation, and preferences of the child; and proactive intervention to assist CWDs in individualized learning to best meet the students' needs.
- **Learning outcomes.** This means setting targets for learning outcomes, combining academic and functional life skills, making adaptation and modification while teaching and learning, and arranging monitoring and assessment using different methods.
- **Learning materials.** Adequate learning materials according to students' needs should be available in different formats and through multiple channels (traditional, online, etc.). Different types of materials are suited for different types of disabilities and possibly also in different local languages.
- **Working in teams of professionals.** Inclusive education means working in partnership and teams with different professionals and specialists to cross-fertilize expertise; and having regular meetings with teachers, parents, health service providers, school psychologists, school nurses, social workers,

assistants, therapists, counselors, among others. The learners with disabilities should always participate when possible.
- **Information and communication technology and assistive devices.** These include the use of digital learning methods and tools to the the learner's specific needs in a pedagogically sound way that supports achievement of the learning outcomes.
- **Additional resources.** The important role of their families and advocacy groups is also used as a valuable resource. Parents should be engaged in supporting the child in learning in inclusive education. It is important to engage with the community at large to enhance the community's awareness about CWDs and the need to support their education process and lifelong learning.

For Children with Disabilities and Their Parents and Families
- **Right to quality inclusive education.** CWDs have the right to inclusive education.
- **Active contribution.** Parents and family are encouraged to actively engage and cooperate with education authorities and schools to arrange teaching and learning according to the individual needs of CWDs.
- **Advocacy.** Parents and family are encouraged to actively contribute and support the development of inclusive education with other partners.
- **Raise awareness.** Parents and family are encouraged to actively contribute and advocate to raise awareness of inclusive education in the community.

For Educators
- **Child-centered approach.** The needs of CWDs are the focus in teaching and learning.
- **Individualized learning.** Curricula and instruction (content, process, outputs) are adapted according to the CWDs' strengths, requirements, and learning styles.
- **Team work.** Plan and agree on the methods of learning differentiation of CWDs in a team (general education teacher or class teacher, special education teacher, parent, etc.).
- **Differentiation of content.** What the child needs to learn according to the adjusted curricula.
- **Differentiation of process.** Preferred methods that support how the CWDs learn best.
- **Differentiation of product.** Learning outcomes (values, knowledge, skills, competencies); how are they presented and demonstrated; and the methods of assessment (national, school, peer and/or self-assessment).
- **Safety and security.** Support policy and necessary guidelines for school's physical facilities that promote safety and security of CWDs.

For the Community
- **Partnerships.** Partnership at the community with parents; caregivers; members of the school bodies like parent–teacher associations and civil society organizations; and members, volunteers, and others in the community.
- **Community activities.** Inclusion into nonformal learning by civil society organizations; recognition of nonformal learning as part of formal learning; and after-school activities for social contacts in hobbies supported by civil society organizations, volunteers, and peers.
- **Safe journeys to school.** Ensuring safety on the way to school and back by the school and/or parents.
- **Advocacy for inclusion.** Raising awareness of community members and society about inclusion in education.

Recommendations

The following recommendations are drawn from the findings and conclusions of the study. The recommendations are provided for the different levels and target groups of education development.

For Individual Learners with Disabilities
- Request learner-centered approach. The learner's needs are the focus in teaching and learning.
- Request individualized learning. Curricula and instruction (content, process, outputs) are adapted according to the learner's strengths, requirements, and learning styles.
- Request differentiation of learning content. What the learner needs to learn according to the adapted curricula.
- Request differentiation of learning process. Preferred methods on learning.
- Request differentiation of product. Learning outcomes (values, knowledge, skills, competencies); how are they presented and demonstrated; and the methods of assessment (national, school, peer and/or self-assessment).

For Governments
- Initiate or embed inclusive education in education policy with sector-wide approach or whole-education approach. The government and/or ministry of education or local level should lead and coordinate the resources toward inclusive education, steering actions and initiating changes in education institutions.
- Adopt the policy of a twin-tracked approach (inclusion in mainstream education and special support for learners with disabilities).
- Coordinate the inclusion in partnerships with all stakeholders (civil society organizations, disability organizations, parents' associations, education specialists and researchers, health specialists) to benefit from the different expertise and resources available.
- Develop a monitoring and evaluation system with clear targets and indicators for achievement and regular follow-up.
- Plan and initiate the collection of disability-disaggregated data (including gender-disaggregated data) to monitor progress regularly, e.g., in EMIS (access, enrollment, retention, levels, transition, graduation, number of trained teachers, support staff, materials, learning environments).
- Secure financial and human resources for the development of inclusive education for CWDs, supported also with donor funding.
- Initiate capacity-building programs at different levels for all staff.
- Develop teacher education programs on inclusive education for general teachers. Acknowledge and provide incentives for teachers who choose to add inclusive education certifications to their credentials.
- Develop special education teacher programs on disability, in general, and specialization on different types of disabilities, in cooperation with universities.
- Initiate curricula reform for adapted curricula with individualized teaching and learning approaches, allowing differentiation of subject context, learning process, and products to the needs of learners with disabilities.
- Prepare a long-term development approach, starting with inclusion from ECEC and primary education, and progressing from one level to another in gradual phases.

- Develop effective mechanisms, support systems, and active measures for transition and progress from one level to another (basic, secondary, TVET, higher education).
- Ensure early screening and assessment in a team of professionals (specialists from health, education, and social fields) to make recommendations for successful inclusion.
- Provide a referral system for families and parents for advice on the rights of CWDs as well as on available services, materials, and resources.
- Advocate for the parents and ensure that CWDs have access to quality inclusive education, complemented with support services.
- Follow closely the international conventions and declarations on education of CWDs; follow up and continue the development and updates in national legislation, policies, and practices of education accordingly.
- Launch campaign and advocacy for inclusive education.

For Schools

- Commit to implementing inclusive education in the school's values, strategies, and practices in teaching and learning.
- Participate in capacity building and training by all education staff (teachers and school staff, members of school bodies, school administration) and introduce new concepts in teaching and learning practice.
- Participate regularly in continued professional development and training of teachers for self-efficacy to embed inclusive education into the practices of teaching and learning.
- Hire special education teachers to support general teachers in inclusive classes.
- Design IEPs for learners according to an adapted curriculum, preferably in a team; and plan learning objectives, areas of learning, methods, timetable, assessment methods, recognition of learning outcomes in terms of knowledge and skills, and feedback.
- Differentiate the instruction by teachers to adopt proactive intervention in the classroom with multilevel lesson planning; differentiate the content, process, and product of learning; consider the readiness, interest strength, motivation, and preferences of the child; and conduct proactive intervention to assist CWDs in individualized learning to best meet the students' needs.
- Set targets for learning outcomes by combining academic and functional life skills, adapt and modify while teaching and learning, and arrange monitoring and assessment using different methods.
- Ensure adequate learning materials for any type of disability according to the learners' needs; and ensure materials in different formats and through multiple channels (traditional, online, radio, etc.)
- Work in partnerships and teams with different professionals and specialists to cross-fertilize expertise. Have regular meetings with teachers, parents, health service providers, school psychologists, school nurses, social workers, assistants counselors, among others. The learners should always participate when possible.
- Work in teams, supported by professionals and specialists who have a key position in securing quality inclusive education for CWDs; benefit from cross-fertilization of expertise.
- Ensure access to ICT and assistive devices for all CWDs in schools, including remote areas. Use digital learning methods and tools according to the learner's specific needs in a pedagogically sound way to support the achievement of learning outcomes.
- Make safety and security policy and protocol for CWDs mandatory in schools. Organize an inclusive learning environment that is safe, functional, and disability-friendly, ensuring accessibility within and outside the school building.

- Benefit from additional human resources and use the important role of families and disability organizations and advocacy groups as a valuable resource; engage the parents to support the child in learning.

For the Communities
- Work in partnership at community level with parents, caregivers, members of the school bodies like parent–teacher associations; civil society organizations; and members, volunteers, and others in the community.
- Develop community activities for inclusive education, e.g., nonformal learning by civil society organizations; recognition of nonformal learning as part of formal learning; and after-school activities for social contacts in hobbies supported by civil society organizations, volunteers, and peers.
- Work with parents, teachers, and community members to enhance lifelong learning for CWDs, but also sensitization on the importance of education for CWDs and children from marginalized and vulnerable groups.
- Ensure safe school trips. Ensuring safety on the way to school and back in the community.
- Advocate for inclusion. Raise awareness of inclusion in education among community members and society.

BIBLIOGRAPHY

Björn, P. M., M. T. Aro, T. K. Koponen, L. S. Fuchs, and D. H. Fuchs. 2016. The many faces of special education within RTI frameworks in the United States and Finland. *Learning Disability Quarterly.* 39 (1). pp. 58–66.

Brossard. 2021. Education Sector Analysis: Methodological Guidelines, Volume 3.

CAST, Inc. Universal Design for Learning.

Center for Parent Information and Resources. 2020. Supports, Modifications, and Accommodations for Students.

Drukpa, U. 2020. Prioritized Curriculum to be used as the New Normal Curriculum henceforth. *The Bhutanese.* 31 October.

Euridyce. n.d. National Education Systems.

Euridyce. 2018. Educational Support and Guidance.

European Agency for Special Needs and Inclusive Education. 2019. Cali Commitment to equity and inclusion in education. 15 October.

European Commission. Eurydice.

Forlin, C., I. G. Cedillo, S. Romero-Contreras, T. Fletcher, and H. J. Rodriguez Hernández. 2010. Inclusion in Mexico: Ensuring supportive attitudes by newly graduated teachers. *International Journal of Inclusive Education.* 14 (7). pp. 723–739.

Forlin, C., C. Earle, T. Loreman, and U. Sharma. 2011. The Sentiments, Attitudes, and Concerns about Inclusive Education Revised (SACIE-R) scale for measuring pre-service teachers' perceptions about inclusion. *Exceptionality Education International.* 21 (3). pp. 50–65.

Forlin, C., N. Kawai, and S. Higuchi. 2015. Educational reform in Japan towards inclusion: Are we training teachers for success? *International Journal of Inclusive Education.* 19 (3). pp. 314–331.

Global Action on Disability (GLAD) Network. 2017. The Network.

Global Disability Innovation Hub. 2018. *Disability Innovation Strategy 2021–2024.* London.

Griful-Freixenet, J., K. Struyven, and E. WendelienVantieghem. 2020. Exploring the interrelationship between Universal Design for Learning (UDL) and Differentiated Instruction (DI): A systematic review. *Educational Research Review.* 29. February.

Halinen, I. and R. Järvinen. 2008. Towards inclusive education: The case of Finland. *Prospects.* 38 (1). pp. 77–97.

Handicap International - Humanity & Inclusion. 2018. Nepal: New Project Empowers Children with Disabilities to Read Confidently. News and press release. 5 May.

―――. 2017. *Nepal: New Project Empowers Children with Disabilities to Read Confidently.*

―――. 2020. *Let's Break Silos Now! Achieving Disability-Inclusive Education in a Post-COVID World.* Luxembourg.

Handicap International, Humanity and Inclusion. 2020. *Let's Break Silos Now.* Luxembourg.

Handicap International, Technical Resources Division. 2012. *Policy Paper: Inclusive Education.* Lyon.

Himalayan Education and Development (HEAD Nepal). Disability Information Advisory Services.

International Disability Alliance. 2021. Global Disability Summit: 2022. 9 June.

Klassen, R. M., V. M. C. Tze, S. M. Betts, and K. A. Gordon. 2011. Teacher efficacy research 1998-2009: Signs of progress or unfulfilled promise? *Educational Psychology Review.* 23 (1). pp. 21–43.

Lawrence-Brown, D. 2004. Differentiated Instruction: Inclusive Strategies for Standards-Based Learning That Benefit The Whole Class. *American Secondary Education.* 32 (3).

Lindner, K. and S. Schwab. 2020: Differentiation and individualisation in inclusive education: A systematic review and narrative synthesis. *International Journal of Inclusive Education.*

Malinen, O. P., H. Savolainen, and J. Xu. 2012. Beijing in-service teachers' self-efficacy and attitudes towards inclusive education. *Teaching and Teacher Education.* 28 (4). pp. 526–534.

Mitchell, D. 2005. Introduction: Sixteen propositions on the contexts of inclusive education. In D. Mitchell. ed. *Contextualizing Inclusive Education: Evaluating Old and New International Perspectives.* London: Routledge. pp. 1–21.

Mitra, S. 2013. A Data Revolution for Disability-Inclusive Development. *The Lancet.* 1 (4). pp. E178–E179.

Moriña, A. 2017. Inclusive Education in Higher Education: Challenges and Opportunities. *European Journal of Special Needs Education.* 32 (1). pp. 3–17.

National Association of Special Education Teachers.

Organisation for Economic Cooperation and Development (OECD) OECD iLibrary. *Who Needs Special Education Professional Development?* (accessed 1 November 2021).

Pratham Every Child in School & Learning Well.

Räty, L., E. Kontu, and R. Pirttimaa. 2016. Teaching children with intellectual disabilities: Analysis of research-based recommendations. *Journal of Education and Learning.* 5 (2). pp. 318–336.

Savolainen, H. 2009. Responding to diversity and striving for excellence: The case of Finland. *Prospects.* 39. pp. 281–292.

Savolainen, H., P. Engelbrecht, M. Nel, and O. P. Malinen. 2012. Understanding teachers' attitudes and self-efficacy in inclusive education: Implications for pre-service and in-service teacher education. *European Journal of Special Needs Education.* 27 (1). pp. 51–68.

Sharma, U., P. Aiello, E. M. Pace, P. Round, and P. Subban. 2018. In-service teachers' attitudes, concerns, efficacy and intentions to teach in inclusive classrooms: An international comparison of Australian and Italian teachers. *European Journal of Special Needs Education.* 33 (3). pp. 437–446.

Sharma, U., T. Loreman, and C. Forlin. 2012. Measuring teacher efficacy to implement inclusive practices. *Journal of Research in Special Educational Needs.* 12 (1). pp. 12–21.

Tomlinson, C. A. 2000. Reconcilable differences? Standards-based teaching and differentiation. *Educational Leadership.* 58. pp. 6–11.

———. 2003. *Fulfilling the Promise of the Differentiated Classroom: Strategies and Tools for Responsive Teaching.* Alexandria, VA: Association for Supervision and Curriculum Development (ASCD).

———. 2014. *Differentiated Classroom. Responding to the Needs of All Learners.* 2nd ed. Alexandria, VA: ASCD.

United Nations. Convention on the Rights of Persons with Disabilities (CRPD).

———. 2006. *Convention on the Rights of Persons with Disabilities and Optional Protocol.*

United Nations Children's Fund (UNICEF). 2021. Mapping of Disability-Inclusive Education Practices in South Asia. Kathmandu, Nepal: UNICEF Regional Office for South Asia.

UNICEF, Kyrgystan. Children with Disabilities.

———. 2018. Improving education opportunities to children with disabilities in the Kyrgyz Republic. Press release. 16 November.

UNICEF, Nepal. 2021. *Reimagining a Better Post-Pandemic World for Children with Disabilities: Conference Proceedings.* 3 December.

UNICEF Data. 2019. *A World Ready to Learn: Prioritizing Quality Early Childhood Education.*

United Nations Educational, Scientific and Cultural Organization (UNESCO). 1994. *The Salamanca Statement and Framework for Action on Special Needs Education.* Paris.

———. 2005. *Guidelines for inclusion: Ensuring Access to Education for All.* Paris.

———. 2009. *Policy Guidelines on Inclusion in Education.* Paris.

———. 2013. The ICT Opportunity for a Disability-Inclusive Development Framework: New action-oriented report. Press release. 23 September.

———. 2017. *A Guide for Ensuring Inclusion and Equity in Education.* Paris.

———. 2018. Education and Disability: Analysis of data from 49 countries.

United Nations General Assembly. 2015. *Transforming our world: The 2030 Agenda for Sustainable Development.* New York.

Vainikainen, M. P., H. Thuneberg, S. Greiff, and J. Hautamäki. 2015. Multiprofessional collaboration in Finnish schools. *International Journal of Educational Research.* 72. pp. 137–148.

BIBLIOGRAPHY

Van Steen, T. and C. Wilson. 2020. Individual and cultural factors in teachers' attitudes towards inclusion: A meta-analysis. *Teaching and Teacher Education.* 95. 103127.

Washington Group on Disability Statistics.

World Health Organization (WHO). 2011. *World Report on Disability.* Geneva.

———. 2016. *Priority Assistive Products List.* Geneva.

World Bank. 2019. *Inclusive Education Initiative: Transforming Education for Children with Disabilities.* Brief. Washington, DC.

www.ingramcontent.com/pod-product-compliance
Lightning Source LLC
Chambersburg PA
CBHW060923170426
43191CB00025B/2463